Lightning Struck Me Twice

Ella Shutze

for you

CONTENTS

Acknowledgments   i

1   Prelude: Genesis   1-3

2   Intro: The Dark Side   4-68

3   Interlude: Abraxas   69-104

4   Outro: The Light Side   105-170

ACKNOWLEDGMENTS

Everyone always says to "love yourself," but very often no one tells you how to do so. I think that's mainly because no one really knows how to love themselves and, if they did, it would be different for everyone. I don't think that we will ever be able to love ourselves completely, and that's okay. If we can wrap our minds around the fact that pain is essential, just as much as love and happiness, then accepting yourself can be easier to grasp a hold of. If you can stop pushing away the pain and instead welcome the hurting with warm arms and let it break you into a million, scattering pieces, then, and only then, may you see your beauty of life.

Ella Shutze

PRELUDE: GENESIS

The linear projector of Light and Dark may seem as if they are stuck at opposite ends of the spectrum with Dark being bad and Light as good. These representations may appear whole, stationary, but in retrospect the Dark and Light are interchangeable - like how a stranger may become a friend, to a lover, and then an enemy in any particular order. What "good" that is marked on the Light side can be turned to "bad" in a different vision or setting. Those events perceived as "bad" may end up transforming us most, thus being a growth aspect on the Light side.

The Light and Dark co-exist inside of us all, neither one more dangerous or liberating than the other; both essential to life.

The Light and Dark side of life that lies inside our souls may seem totally out of reach and scary, but to experience **both pain and ecstasy** is to be as alive as possible.

i hope you experience despair and pain and live through it, so that you may then experience love and happiness and can have truly known the world's existence:

a life of color.

INTRO: THE DARK SIDE

I did this to myself.

I hold onto the devil's hand. I clutch his staff in my hands and puncture my own self. He covers my eyes with his crimsoned blindfold in which he calls love and holds me in his grasps - with the angel behind me. Caught in a lie, I forget what it feels like to truly feel alive. I am self-possessed by the demon, self-obsessed by the sin. With a final cold breath, the devil pushes me forward. I see my hope of a bright future disappear; the devil is leading me on the wrong path. The angel - now hesitating in front of me. I reach forward, but the enemy's glove is glued onto my hand. I shout for help, but the devil took my words along with my light. The devil's cracked lips are now on mine. I feel the harsh reality pierce my body with every motion I try to pull away. My pupils are reflecting the light, but I am looking at the dark. The enemy marks my sins on my arm in permanent ink. The demon is now apart of me; the angel - now a pile of ashes on the floor. I am now the villain in this place. Under this mask, I am now a monster.

I was such a fool; now I am the evil.

my mind is Alcatraz, and i cannot swim.

my mother always told me to be careful
of boys with nice smiles
and girls who act out from jealousy,
but she never warned me about
myself.

like everyone else around me,
i too have sculpted a mask that hides
who i truly am.
i too have become a master magician
at alluding my feelings.
i too have become a zoo tamer,
taming my smile to be on for others
when i only want to
scream inside.

do not drabble in the shallow end,

D

  I

    V

      E

        into the deep

sometimes,
i even forget the reason
behind my smile given to others so
automatically.

sometimes,
i even question who i would be if i could give
you love without having to pretend.

our love was a broken kaleidoscope
in a room of a thousand lights.

the little kid asks the smoker for a lighter,
and the old man tells the kid that
smoking is not healthy.
yet, the man continues to smoke,
because he's convinced he is too long-gone
to survive now.

you started with my grandmother, building a dark home
in her lungs,
at least that's what they told me.
because you took her life before i started mine,
leaving a whole smoky city in the place where she once
effortlessly breathed.
are you happy now?

you soon took my friend's dad, writing your name all
over his colon.
then, you had the audacity to get my mom.
you first visited her for a year when i was 8 but got bored
and left.
but you couldn't help it, you loved the taste of her and
came back for more.
you barged in before knocking-
this time building a permanent, large home by the name
of stage four.
by that time, it was too late to tear your deathly mansion
down with medicine,
so you took her from me.

i heard you like little kids too; it's been all over the news.
what heartbreaking stories to hear you took their life
away before they even had the chance to understand this
beautiful, harsh world.
are you happy now?
now that you're known all over the world?

you tear people's worlds apart.

it's no secret you kill.

you've taken away millions of lives.
when will you finally stop these silent crimes?
you've made a whole family that takes over every part of
the body.
will time eventually erase you to be left in the medical
history books?
when will this end?
will someone find a cure?
or will you be unbeatable till eternity,

forevermore?

i spent an eternity giving you my heart,
and you threw it back.
in shattered pieces.
in a mere second.

Ella Shutze

the Waffle House flirts
with the Coffee Shop,
and the Smoothie Store cries.

he loved her so much that he forgot about himself.

before i met him,
i was scared of everything.
now the only thing i am scared of
is myself when i'm with him.

If I close my eyes, will it all go away?
Or will the Monsters chase me in my dreams too?
If I go, is there a guarantee that my suffering will end?

I don't want to go, but I have no more hope.
I don't want to do this, but I have no other place to run to
where I can feel loved.
This isn't a game anymore.
I have turned into an abandoned aeroplane with no
engine and fuel;
I can't go up.
I'm stuck in rock bottom.
I don't know how to climb out.
Trust me, I've tried *everything*.
You were the only one who could pull me out.

I wish I could see you right now.

So I'll end it all for you, for us.
And maybe up there, the Monsters will turn into Angels.

I have to at least find out.

if this is the last time our eyes will meet,
i want to remember what it feels like to look into your
soul filled with beautiful sparks.
if this is the last moment i shall hear your laugh,
i want to remember the way it electrifies my whole body
like no lightning strike could ever do.
if this is the last time our hearts will ever be near each
other,
i want to remember how it feels to know that i am not
alone.
if this shall be the last time our hands intertwine,
then i want to memorise the lines on your palms,
so i can trace them on my heart whenever i feel lost,
hoping it will lead me back to you.

when you cry, i will cry.
because i love you.
because i hurt for you.

i know your language is hate,
but i can only explain it to you in love.

he never felt like home, because home wasn't supposed to feel trapped and overwhelming. it wasn't supposed to make you go crazy, but he always did.

the thing about putting yourself in someone else is that you give them the keys and at any time they can lock you in. and you are stuck in the pain that you created, with no (visible) escape.

I'm falling further away.
I am tired of always being tired.
Help me get out of this.
Please,
let this go away.
Why won't this go away?
Is this the world's punishment?

Help me.

Save me.

Someone.

Anyone.

Please.

i didn't prepare for landing,

so i

CRASHED

sometimes you must lie to get to the truth,

even if it hurts.

"You are not sad. How could you possibly be sad when I see you smiling everyday? When I see you making others laugh, making them feel better about their own pain? You have no right to feel lonely when all you have are people lined up wanting to talk to you," they said.
"You could not possibly feel empty when you have high marks in your classes, a complete family, and friends." they said.

But they were wrong. He had felt so lonely and left out, no one to turn to, no one who understood him and his way of thinking.
He was so lost: a simple, radiant boy on the outside, but a treacherous never-ending maze on the inside.

- he had every right to feel those emotions

your heart is meant to beat for yourself and you only,
not anyone else.

live for yourself.

so bottle me up and pull me in.
put me on the shelf and let me age,
because the older i am the better i taste?
the smell of whiskey on your breath-
you grab towards me with your drunken, messed-up
mind.
how can you live like this?
how have you never learned that no matter how much
you take in, the next morning is just going to be worse?
baby, the more you do it, the more you lose.
the late nights you drive, i try to warn you but every time
you still risk a life of innocent children and mature minds
at the fault of your hazy mind.
but someday it won't end well.
you'll swerve too soon, because you were too careless,
and i won't be there to save you.

you offer me some, but how many times do i have to tell
you?
i do not solve my problems by consuming drinks.
my god, don't you know this kills?
this ruins hearts, and this ruins minds, but you still do it
anyways, despite my countless cries for you to
just stop.

baby, i am not wine.
i was not made for your pleasure.
i am not the rum whom you run to when you need a
break from the outside world.

i am not the beer that you show off to your friends

and take pride in how much you have.
i am not the moonshine you like to wrap your fingers
around and get wasted on countless of times.

a little bit is never enough for you.
please stop indulging in me,
i am not your safe haven.
i am not just something you can consume on a daily
basis.
baby, **i am not the empty broken glasses shattered
across your hardwood floor.**

you've overdosed on drinks and pills.
you've overdosed on the idea of wanting me,
yet you won't admit it.
but every time you walk, you stumble.
and i can see the audacity in your eyes: never wanting
this high to end.
baby, i will not be able to save your worries now,
so please stop reaching towards me.
eventually this high will end, and when it does you can't
keep going for more and more and more,
because your money is almost out and your friends have
all left you.
darling, there is no more.

at least not from me,

anymore.

even if it pains me, i will keep giving you my strength

Ella Shutze

i say, "i'm through."
and you say "me too."
but the truth is:
i'll never stop loving you.

he is upside down, but the rest of the world is in place.

i have loved others with all of my heart
that when i needed some for myself,
there wasn't any more love i could hold.

with a great love comes a great sorrow, a hurting pain
beyond measures that (love)
: something so beautiful and vibrant :
could turn to something so terrifying and treacherous.

-what great pain to know that great love
must eventually end,
too.

every nightmare starts off as a dream.

"but i love you; isn't that all that matters?" she asked him, begging for him to stay.

there's a long pause in which if you were to take one step into that room, you would physically feel the hurt between the two (past) lovers.

"sometimes love isn't enough. sometimes it is not the answer that will fix everything," he said, with a look of sorrow in his mud-brown eyes. "sometimes taking care of yourself is more important than the love you have built up inside of you for another. and (sometimes) love cannot save you." voice shaking, he continued,
"love cannot save us this time."

when she looked up at him, a pool of tears forming in her pixie-dust eyes, he hesitated before saying anything else. he quickly looked away, not being able to handle what he was doing to her.
but, hoping that she would listen to him, he took a slow breath, holding in everything he ever loved about her and letting it out through his mouth.

"i'm sorry, but i cannot save you this time; only *you* can do that. i'm sorry. sometimes love for others ruins you when you do not love yourself."

with his last attempt to consolidate his feelings, he held her cold, trembling hands, looked into her now puddled eyes and whispered into her hurting ear:
"love yourself, so that we can come together again."

and then he left her sitting there with his words echoing in her mind.

love yourself, so that you can love me.

you see,
i never lie to people,
but i lie to myself when looking in the mirror.

why is that?

you looked at her like she was a beautiful, delicate flower
in a sea of shining diamonds, and you always loved
flowers more than jewels.

she looked at you like you were just another picture in a
sea of pretty sculptures of bodies, and she always loved
the sculptors more than the photographers.

you'd see her walk by like she was the wind and
everything revolved around her, and you always
preferred the wind to the fire.

and she?

she doesn't even notice the beautiful hurricane you carry
around on the back of your broad shoulders, my love,
but i always have.

here's the thing about constantly being in second place:
it isn't bad, but it will drive you mentally mad.
because you're pushed to the side like the friend of a
bride.
it's social suicide and constant disappointment,
because you grew up learning that it was not as
important.
they tell you no one pays attention to the silver,
only the true winner.
and yes, i know it's all too familiar.
i know you have never gotten the taste of "true" victory,
and your name is not written in history or important
enough to be in a documentary.
i know it's the same people who always beat you,
but please know that a medal will not complete you.
please, don't let this defeat you.
yes, i know the people on top never seem to stop.
the momentum they've built seems higher than the tallest
rooftops.
but don't let this defeat you; let it create you.

you see, the thing about always getting second place is
that it leaves you feeling like a disgrace,
you feel as if you're in the wrong place.
because no one ever congratulates you;
when they reach out their hands it goes right past you to
the person who outlasted you.
you keep chasing the gold and eventually, it's going to

get old. you're told no one ever remembers the person
who got second in the long run,
but believe me -

you're not the only one who was outrun
by what feels like everyone.

stop.
before i indulge in an overdose of your touch
stop. you know my secrets aren't good enough
stop.
before this gets too much
you know i can't handle this stuff

stop.

i told you to leave,
but you're my disease-
my cure when you want to be

restart: "everyone suffers in their life,"
at least that's what you told me
you know i want you babe
you know i need you by my side
or else i won't survive

stop.
you're my fatal disease
but you know your lips are my cure
stop.
think about your family, think about your future before
you go any further
stop.
who let you think the world revolves around you?
i drew the line but you crossed that too
i guess my boundaries are nothing to you
people are saying "that's just how it is, you don't get to
choose"

stop.
they don't know the half

stop.
you're like an addiction to me
and you know i can't quit
can we calm things down a little? maybe slow down a
little?
stop. i already told you no
i have places to go
stop.
i scream out but no one hears me
no matter what they say i'm still not free

if you call me a liar, then you'll be the liar
stop.

reverse.

love makes no mistake, only the person.

i loved you in pieces.

i fell in love with your soul first.
then not long after,
your sea-foam green eyes overtook my mind.

soon after that, my eyes came to admire your boxed
smile, and then everything else you had to offer came to
my heart in waves.

never all at once, though.

maybe that's why i couldn't love all of you at once.
maybe that's why i could never fully love you.
because you were a puzzle in which each individual piece
was its own piece of art;
but, once solved-
once put together,
you were not a masterpiece,
but merely a mask,
hiding all your beautiful pieces from the world.

you were a highway that i traveled on for 4 years.
i always saw the exit signs but ignored them.
i kept going, despite the multiple opportunities to leave.
i didn't know it back then,
but i was headed towards a fire.
i could've taken a different way, but i chose your path.
i chose to follow your veins like a map of this highway
that you are.

you were broken roads that needed repairing.
and because you were not whole, you made others crack
too.

when i reached the fire on the road, it destroyed me.
the smoke a few miles ahead should have been enough to
warn me, but i didn't pay much attention.
and i should've changed lanes sooner when i saw the
fire-trucks rush by, but for some reason i kept going.

when i reached the fire, i saw her car.
i should've known it when i saw her Blue Maserati come
racing onto the scene, but i didn't because i was too
focused on you.

little did i know at the time that she would be the reason
for the fire to have escalated.
that the roaring fire was all because of her piercing, Blue
car.
little did i know at the time that after 4 years of me
memorising your twisting, winding, and manipulating
roads, that this would all end in flames because of a girl
you cheated on me with, and her Blue car.

you were a highway that i traveled on for 4 years.

i always thought your least favorite color was Blue,
but I guess you loved her shade of teal.

i didn't know it back then, but i was headed towards a
heartbreak from a guy who lied to me about a girl in a

Blue Maserati.

i soon became invisible to those around me. they only noticed me when they needed help. they took advantage of my brain and kind heart. no one ever thought of how that made me feel, though. so i soon became everyone's last choice; the one they went to when no one else was there. do you know what it feels like to always be there for others and have them not be there for you and push you away? do you know how it feels to put on a smile and still be hated on? do you know what it feels like to be surrounded by sad people and still be happy? do you know what it feels like to be the only survivor of this Hell?

do you know how it feels to be the sun invisible to all those in the dark?

as much as i need you,
i'm worried the world is covetous of us.
i'm scared because of what we have
that fate will betray us.

what then?

what if our love is so praised that the future messes it up?
because the future hates us:
those who figure things out,
those who oppose all oppositions and continue on.

the milky-way is jealous of us,
i know it all too well,
and this love will eventually come to wreck us.

what then?

i'm worried the spirits envy us.
i'm worried because of what we have,
it will all be torn apart.

i would bury all my pain
so you wouldn't suffer from my suffering.

i would put my disguise on
so you could be inspired.

i'd break a thousand times
and hide it all away.

for you

all this hating and words just repeating-
used to hurt feelings and hands shake not because it's
freezing outside.
you don't understand how words can leave such pain
about the weight that you gain and not having a "smart
enough" brain;
like i've been dealt the ace of spades but was then
betrayed,
words and i are constantly in a battle -
one i'll never win because this world can never be the
same after all these spoken sins.

people always tell you how to behave
and in schools, they have you learn from textbooks about
science and war's alliance
but not about how to be a good person
or what you should do when the world feels like it's
crashing in on you.

people don't understand how powerful words can be.
they just think it's spoken debris and that life is carefree.
shots, pills, and yes, drinking kills...
but words?
words can grow people apart, make them fall apart, think
they're not a work of art.
but words?

they can also make people more smart, understand each
other from heart to heart, make them want to take part in
something bigger than themselves.
words can be art, not just a silence filler
because you don't like the dinner or that she was the
winner and not you.

the world is not your stage; i don't care if you're from the
elizabethan age.
the world is a cage full of dark hearts on a rampage.
people lie and suddenly say goodbye,
and life is not always a clear blue sky.
people still look at your color and how many times you
pray a day.
don't tell me people can just become new men
and save the world from a war like Harry S. Truman.

**the monsters don't live under your bed, they live in
the words you have said, telling people you wish they
were dead.**
**but the angels don't live in the sky, they float in the
words you've cried, trying to save those who wish to
say goodbye.**

violence is not the answer, but we use it anyways.
words are not always the answer, but we should use the
good ones anyways.

i reach for you,
but you aren't there.

you aren't here.

I live in fear of what I do not know
I hide from things I cannot understand
I scream alone,
but the monsters scream back,
louder
I sleep scarcely, afraid of the dark
Afraid of myself, I cracked the mirror
I dream a dream so big that others think
I cannot work for it
I am lost
Those I used to know disown me
There is a crack on my face,
which will only get deeper the more I go on like this

So I put a mask on to hide my broken pieces,
because everything worthy of beauty is whole,

right?

the thing blocking the sunshine today is your worries about the clouds tomorrow.

if there's a place out there called home,
i haven't found it yet.

he wants to love you; you can let him.
but be careful to not let it get to your head.
because the wrong "love" can turn you into something
you are not.

she wants you to trust, so you can choose to trust.
but do not forget that anyone is capable of a lie.

they try to hurt you with their words, so you can let them
hurt you.
but do not let them take over your mind to make you
think you can hurt yourself.

you want to talk to yourself; let your mind wander.
but please do not let your mind only talk about the
bitterness of this world.

your friends want you to change; you can let them
change you.
but do not forget who you are.
if they want to hold you, you can let them hold you.
but do not let their grasps become your safety net.

your parents want to help you, so you are allowed to let
them help.
do not let them end up doing it for you.
because sometimes help from the wrong person is not the
help you need.

they do not want anything to do with you, so you can let them ignore you.
and they want to walk with you, so you can let them walk with you.
but do not let them guide you in the wrong direction.

because even a snake pit can look like a rose garden from the outside.

we were magnets attracting towards each other,
but there was a stronger force pulling us apart.

you left, before you even arrived

even on the bright days,
i still cannot recognise myself - the one that weeps in the
dark.

what tragic sickness - to have everything you ever
wanted in life but not to have known yourself.

rain can still pour when the sun is out.

you can still hurt when you're shinning.
.

her scars are the color of the sky,
so no one recognises them until it's too late.
because they all think scars and bruises are the
color of mud.

i hate you because you left me,
but i hate myself even more
because i went
after you.

i can't sleep.

i'm scared my thoughts will become too much
for my body to handle that it'll give up
before morning.

I am surrounded by the dark side; its name is Narcissism.

He looked like a pond from the outside,
but when I stepped in, he was an ocean,
and I do not know how to swim.
This is not how I want to live anymore.
The dark side has put a mask over my mouth,
filtering out all the good.
He has sculpted me a map that leads me the wrong way.
I am now lost on the dark side.

Can anyone hear me?
Or has the devil taken you too?

INTERLUDE: ABRAXAS

I close my eyes and try to imagine what my life would be like if you had not arrived and everything is still. No chaos, no heartbreak and questions, just a linear mirage. But, at the same time, everything is also lonely and boring and dull. Every thrilling feeling of beauty and love has disappeared. Do you think it is worth it to give up heartbreak and have no love in return?

Do you think protecting yourself from danger is still good even if you can't live freely?

I'd build myself new again for you if that's what you
wanted. I'd build a whole universe for you,
if you asked.

maybe we'll meet again 4 years from now, somewhere in a coffee shop down the small street where we first met. and maybe i'll tell you how nice you look, and you'll tell me how much i have changed, yet that my smile is still the same one you came to love.

maybe one of us will confess that we still have feelings for the other, or maybe we won't.
we'd just look at each other: our eyes searching into each other's, trying to catch up on four years of missed information.
just two friends, who were once in love (and who maybe still are) looking at each other for a long, long time.

maybe you'll tell me about the girl you met with whom you want to marry. and i'll smile, telling you that "i am glad you found the one. i am glad you are happy, even if it isn't because of me."

and we'll just smile at each other, two people who were once one just standing there, looking into each other's eyes, and asking one another if they still love them.

maybe the answer will be yes, but maybe we won't admit it. and we'll just be two souls who fell in love too fast, too young, without any warning.

and then maybe we'll part ways once again, with unanswered questions of what we mean to each other now- after 4 years of wondering.

and with our words of goodbye, maybe we'll know how
the other one feels: that after all this time, we still haven't
forgotten each other.

and we'll just be two strangers who were once in love,
(and who maybe still are) just existing on earth,
wondering if we will ever find that type of love again.

don't you think everyone,
at least for one moment in their life,
wishes they were someone else?

the bright days will come,
but for now i have to keep on going;
i have to keep on believing.

if you take a walk in someone's shoes,
you'll only know where they are going,
not where they have been in the past.
and the past is what shapes us.
so, go ahead, walk in their shoes,
but don't forget that that isn't all to someone.

if rain descends down 9 meters per second,
how fast would i have to dream,
run,
exist,
to find myself again?

how fast would i have to fall to awaken?

they brought a gun to a peace fight.

-so don't expect me to just sit there and pretend like there is nothing i can do to save this world.

1. how come asking such a personal question of how someone is, is so casual and overlooked?

2. follow up question: how come i can't answer fine and have people think i'm not fine when i actually really am?

3. if there's such thing as a daydream, is there such thing as a nightmare in the daytime too? or is there no name for it, because we're already living in one?

4. can you have a story without an ending? or does it eventually have to end?

5. are we all trying to forget someone, or are we just trying to forget why we were so dependent upon them?

if the whole world loved each other than would it still be love? or would it just be normal?

is giving up the hate and violence worth it for also giving up the feeling of love and peace?

i fear that you will not be here in my arms
when i wake up.

give me your pain,
and i'll give you my love.

we have been apart for so long;
we have drifted across a thousand seas,
yet we are still in this.

-no amount of being apart could pull me from you

"there are so many people whom i don't want to let down and disappoint," i told him.

"i know," he says. " but sometimes, sometimes you just have to do what's best for you and not worry about who you need to impress and satisfy."

"no one will ever be completely satisfied with you but that does not mean that they don't take pride in knowing you. nor does that mean that they don't love you any less." he continued.

- as long as you keep living and being exactly who you are, you won't let others down, at least not in their heart

Above my city, I feel free.
If I can't soar like a bird at least this flight has company.
I'm alone but surrounded by people.
The sky looks so big. The sky is apart of me;
I am the wings.
I can't fly for much longer, but I hope this never ends.
I want to fly high,
but I hope my head does not get lost in the clouds.
This world is not so far away now,
even though I am miles up.
The line between the city and the clouds;
the line between dreams and my reality.
I'm stuck. I can't go up or down.
I'm not the pilot of this plane.
I have to have trust in this flight,

in my fate.

and in the deep darkness of the storm,
the lightning that lit up the whole world
struck me

the electrification hurt like no pain
i have ever felt before,
but from the pain came a new beginning

the lightning then disappeared,
leaving the world in a pitch black state of pain,
and as if the first one was not enough,
lightning struck me a second time -
it felt like pure death,
but i was really being born again

life is like the weather… no matter how many storms or hurricanes and disasters there are, it never ceases to amaze me at how beautiful the weather can appear the next day, hour.

- there will be shattering, destroying storms, but the sun will never fail to rise again, more beautiful than before

land started off as one piece,
then slowly broke out.
but despite its cracks,
it is still magical.

words can touch people like bodies do.

i feel bad for those who do not like surprises and risk taking –
for life is only built from them.

the fireflies here are amazing.
they light up the night sky like no light
or building could ever do.
each night i count them the way
i count down the days till
i can love myself.

love for ourselves?

it would never be enough,
but it would also be more liberating and transformative
than anything ever before.

in a faraway town, there is a broken-winged butterfly whose light cries could not even be heard by a dog centimeters away.

the butterfly has no-one whom she can turn to for help. a light breeze shifts her focus to the sky - thousands of birds with much bigger, sturdier wings than hers, soaring above. how she wishes she could be one. how she wishes the world could see her like the other birds up there.

but in her small corner of her home, she is unaware of how loved her existence is. how people love to look at gatherings of those just like her. how kids gape at the light catching off of her wings.

she cries for what she wishes to be, but she does not know how much she is appreciated.

she does not know.

i remember what it was like looking at my heart compared to others and remembering what it was like to truly feel

alone.

show them that you are so much more than what
they think you are.

-you are a warrior not just a worrier

"forever?" he says, skeptical of the word's meaning. "forever is a long time."

"no," i tell him. "forever isn't nearly enough time."

May 10, 2007:

I visit a kindergarten classroom to help fulfill my 20 service hours needed for school. The kids all look so happy to see me. All their wild wonder fills the air like it's all that matters. This is an age where they don't care. Personalities are beginning to grow, and they don't yet understand the importance of school. I watch as they run around, some chasing each other while others pretend to be superheroes.

"Miss," one of them asks me…. " how come you're not playing superhero with us?"

I smile and tell him, "Because I am no superhero."

Seeing the confusion in his face, he doesn't yet know that what I get on a test determines the rest of my future; he doesn't yet know that I do not save people's lives and that running can't fix all of my problems. As time passes and I say my goodbyes, the kids all surround me, not caring that they have sticky fingers and messed up hair.

"Miss?" a girl with curly brown hair asks me "Why can't you stay longer?"

I look into her wild brown eyes and say, "I must go back to studying so I can get a good job."

I watch her big eyes become small; she fears she won't be like this forever. She fears she must get a good job too. As I'm about to head out the door, the teacher asks me to give one piece of advice to the still energetic kids. I pause for a moment and tell them to "have fun." I don't tell them that in ten years they'll be in high school. I don't tell them that they won't be able to run free all the time, that there won't be recess to run wild in the wind. I don't tell them they will encounter nights that will seem like it will never be day. I don't tell them that they will struggle and find hardships in people and in learning. I don't tell them that it all goes by so quickly, that when they're my age they'll wish to be a kid again. I don't give them advice on how to survive older kids and letters that define your intelligence. And I don't tell them how life only gets harder. But something tells me they already know what's coming. As I leave, my mind races with flashes of what their life will be in ten years; I hope they are ready.

-because I am still not

his heart was as dark as my pale-moonlight skin

if you were to take a bite out of the Earth, at first, it'd be
bitter. you'd hate it and would want it to go away, but if
you hang on and let the taste sink in, it'd be sweet, and
you'd only want more.

when the world is tough and you don't like it,
hang on, because it gets better.

whether you know who you are or not, let us walk a road
of strength and companionship.
let us share in the depths of pain and ache.

let us make it together.

death is not a loss in itself; if we didn't lose people in this life, then we would never know the value of life.

- life is so precious, and we have death to remind us of that

i grew the whole world and rebuilt myself for your liking
entirely.

but now,

i have lost my everything,

and it was all for you.

Every fall, the trees all shed their leaves.
After having nothing to cover themselves up with in the winter, they then start fresh with the vibrant pigments of spring.
Each year the cherry blossoms sprout petals more beautiful than before, after going through months of reflection.

Can't I do the same?

OUTRO: THE LIGHT SIDE

Because I spent so much time on the dark side, so much time being a monster, the Devil himself is now afraid of me. Seeing how much I have grown from the dark, the Devil wants to let me go. He knows he has done his job. He knows he has changed my world for the better.

The Devil is now behind me, the Angel- now in my reach again. Holding onto the Devil's hand, I step forward, reaching for the light that is no longer dimming in front of me. The light now captures me. The Devil nods at the Angel, letting him know that I have survived the deepest oceans, the most dangerous storms, and that, now, I am finally ready. The Angel nods back as if to say that he knows the dark side was essential for me to then experience this light.

I was such a fool, but I would have been more of a fool if I had not lived in the dark. I would have been more of a fool if I had not let myself feel the pain.

you see, the dark is all around us; it's apart of us all. take a walk on the dark side, but live on the light. experience the pain, and experience the beauty. become the devil, and then re-birth to the better. so that you may know both pain and ecstasy and grow from both.

so that you may live on the equilibrium of life.

insecurity is inevitable.

but if we can realise that it is also universal,
figure out a way to lift the stigma of it being a weakness,
then those degrading feelings we have on ourselves can
then be seen as a tool for self-growth and love.

breathe.

let the wind carry your worries away.
lift your palm out to the sky.
feel the sun's rays glistening along the creases in your
delicate fingers.
take off your jacket.
let the cold air rush around your skin like a plant so
desperate for water.
let it cleanse you;
allow it to overtake your thoughts
and then let your mind go.
do not hold back;
let yourself go, just for one moment.
look up to the sky.
look at the grey clouds
and feel the rain pour down on your scarred face.
let the raindrops dance on your eyelids like they are apart
of you.
take off your shoes.
let the snow freeze your toes until they are almost numb,
and let everything go.
let the weather wash you clean.
carry the sun in your hands; let the wind brush through
your hair like it was made to do,
welcome the coldness on your arms like family,
make the rain consume you and the snow build you.
feel everything and anything;
just let your mind go.
and just for a moment,

breathe.

open your eyes to the beauty that's been
in front of you all along.
open your heart and find the answer.

Ella Shutze

there's a reason why Advil
does not work on heartaches,
because they were meant to be felt.

she looked at me with brokenness in her eyes,
only visible to those who looked for it,
which anyone only rarely did.

her hands were all bandaged from the bleeding of words,
but if you didn't look closely,
it just looked like scratches from her two cats.

when she would smile, her teeth could be seen coated in
the lies she would tell herself
whilst standing in front of her mirror;
of course, to anyone else, it would seem as if she just had
too white teeth,
but i knew.
i always knew the hurting inside of her,
because that was once me.

maybe one day she too will come to realise her beauty,
her worth.
she just has to find it in her,
and once she finds it,
she will never be the same.
maybe once she loves herself,
she will look back on those younger than she;
and, like me, she will see a part of her in them
and will want to save them.
but she will know that she cannot save them,

because *only they can save themselves.*

you only lose if you think you've lost.

over this dusty mountain, i was thrown.
tell me: how did i land so low?

are you and i the same?

i run to you, lost in this river we created.
i pulled myself out,
whilst you went swimming.

tell me, if this is not what i should do.

tell me: who were you before your parents
and the world told you who to be?

you can't win everything,
but you also can't lose everything.

the truth i hid soon became a lie i told.

i say "i love you too" but really, it's more than love.
it's a feeling so strong that words fail me.
yet, i still say "i love you too,"
because there isn't enough time, not nearly enough words
in the universe to explain how i feel towards you.

i love you too, but it's so much more than that.

                                      it's so much more than love.

you know my language well, but hers was the first language that landed on your tongue. the language of love or English i don't quite know, but i know you could do great things in mine.

you know my city well, but hers was the first place you laid eyes on. the farms of your culture or my streets of danger, i don't know which one is worse, but i know you would be safe in my heart.

if there is one thing i know about your home being 7,000 miles away from mine, is that this is not in my hands anymore. i cannot make you stay. and no matter how much time i spend studying your language, your culture, i cannot make you notice me.

i cannot force this.

he loved himself for who he was,
not for who he wanted to become.

take a look at yourself and ask yourself what have you
done for yourself?

have you lived the life you wanted, or are you living in
the world people have created for you?

is what you've done been for yourself or only to please
others?

have you been trapped in a place that you hand-crafted
yourself?

today, i'm scared.
today, i hope for better days;
tomorrow, i'll hope for a better past.
in the future, i still want to have hope
that will carry me to where i need to be.
in the past, i wish i had that belief in myself.
today, i am alone.
today, i hope for company;
tomorrow i'll hope for individuality.
in the future, i still want to have myself.
in the past, i wish i had that ability to walk alone.
today, i'm tired of talking,
but tomorrow i may be tired of being silenced.
today, i am distraught,

but tomorrow

will not be

today.

the wrong love, the artificial love, can burn like leaves in your precious heart.

love is more painful than pain itself.

smiling or crying, i shall think of you.

I do not know who I am.
I do not know where, or when, I lost myself but it was somewhere between loving you and the line where dreams meet reality.
I got so caught up in the mere thought of you that I forgot to think about myself.
I forgot who I was and who I wanted to become.
I forgot the world, my own existence, because all I wanted to remember was you.
All I needed to remember was you.
My parents drifted away from me, leaving me stuck in Space, saying I was careless with my life.
They tried to pull my lost mind back into the spaceship by counseling, but the lack of gravity was too strong.
My sister and parents soon left me too, along with the rest of life.
Everything except you was out of my mind's reach, because you were all I focused on.
"how can she love him and he doesn't even know her?"
"why does she spend her days wasting away by some guy?"
"he'll never love you; you don't even love or know yourself."
Were all engraved by people in the roots of my floating bones.

I am not forgetful with my life now.
I am not careless with the love I have inside anymore.

I have been pulled back to Earth by a long, twisted rope
of hope.

I am not a stranger to myself anymore.
And my bones are now strung back together with their
roots engraved with the assurance of who I am.
I was lost, but I am now found thanks to you for letting
me drift off.

For when I had nothing in Space,
my mind just floating somewhere in the galaxy,
I found my beautiful self written in the stars.
I was lost, but I am found now.

Love is NOT all you need. No, you also need pain and
hate so you can grow. If you just had love then it
wouldn't be love. It'd be average,
and love isn't average.

all the love and kindness he gave
finally came back to him 10 years later.

our love for ourselves should be as strong as that of others.

maybe life wasn't supposed to be figured out.

maybe life was just supposed to be lived,
to be experienced and cherished for what it is.

hurt
until you bleed
cry
until you cannot breathe,
and make this storm turn into the sun

break until you crack;
then rise,
stronger than before

love is walking the long way to class in the cold just to see a glimpse of them. love is hurting and bleeding. love is crying in your pillow at night because they like someone else. love is waking up at 2 a.m. to catch an 11-hour flight just to see them for 3 hours. love is standing on the beach looking out at the wide, blue ocean and realising how big and great this world is. love is drinking hot chocolate by the fire at night when you can't go to sleep. love is pouring your heart out and getting left despite your endless giving. it's holding the door open for people, even when you don't feel like it. love is healing and torturing. the moment when you realise that in that moment you are truly happy. love is hoping and wishing, breaking and tearing.
love is simple and complicated.

love is love.

love is life, but so is pain.

Ella Shutze

though my eyes do not know you yet,
my heart does because we were made to hurt togther.

-soulmate

if you were to tell me that ten years from now
i will have accomplished my dreams
and have whatever i want in life,
i wouldn't believe you.
because i would've done it in five years.

he looked at her like he was a stargazer going blind,
looking at the stars for the last time.

she was convinced that life was so much more than what
she had been seeing it as,
so she transformed into something so much more than
what others saw her as.

the peach judges the blueberry because it's too thin and the blueberry judges the watermelon because it's too fat. the kiwi is too hairy, and the mango is too bright of it's color. yet, we don't care what the fruits look like; we just care about how they taste, what's on the inside.

"how do you know when you've accepted yourself?"

"well, i think it's different depending on a lot of things, but maybe when you look in the mirror and see your heart as the beauty looking back at you and not your face. maybe, when you love yourself, you don't have the guilt that comes with not being able to see yourself as others do, that you just feel the beauty."

The Devil does not make you sin; he does not force you to punish yourself for the mistakes you have made.

He climbs inside your head and slowly manipulates your mind. He crawls down to your heart and gently squeezes it with envy, leaving a black-inked handprint with a scent of greed on a once innocent organ. He messes with your vision and turns your world side-ways.
Overtime, this becomes your new reality. At anytime you could have stopped; pushed him away, but temptation was stronger to stay.

The Devil never forced you to sin;
he just guided you to his side so you could become *stronger*.

for orange juice to be in its best condition to drink, it must first be shaken.

same goes for you.

Ella Shutze

she cut her hair short,
because people thought
it was most beautiful long.

Dear Newborn,

Welcome to Earth. It's nice here; I'm sure it won't take you long to figure that out. You are going to grow old here. You are going to learn how to walk, talk, play, share, give, and so, so much more. But most importantly: you will learn how to love and how to give out love. You will experience so much, so much that I cannot tell you in words how much you will go through, how much you will experience. You will be on top of the world some days, but you will also fall multiple times and sometimes to a point where all it feels like is that you're losing. Whether you choose to get up and try again is up to you, but you mustn't let failure and defeat get to you or stop you from *anything*. You must hold your friends and family close. You must love them with all of your heart, because they will not be here to protect you forever. There will be days where the whole world seems completely against you. Days where you just feel like giving up and lying in bed forever. But these days it is essential that you must believe in better times, because they will come. My god they will come; you will make so many friends. You will go so many places, and you will end up exactly where you are meant to be. Maybe not at first, you may not even know what you want to do in the future until it is the future, but the universe is magical. My child, it knows what's best for you and it will always look after you. But this world cannot always protect you. You will come crashing down and you will lose; there is no escaping loss. You came into this world for a reason. You will change this world even if it doesn't make it in the news.

And you will make an impact here, one-way or the other. This life was meant for you. You will lose people and people will lose you, but you are meant to be here just as much as everyone else. People are dependent upon you and you are dependent upon others; I hope someday you come to realise that. I hope someday you come to realise why you were brought into this world, because, darling, you were made to change this world.

Love,
Life

through hurting together,
they kept each other alive.

even a wooden pencil cannot stay sharp and strong
forever,
so why should you feel the need to?

by the end of your life i hope you find the beauty in
yourself and in this life.
i hope you find the good in people.

-even if it takes forever

even if it was all in vain,
i'm glad i left you.
i'm glad i had the courage
to finally break free from the dark shackles.

-you shouldn't pick up a broken piece of glass if you
know the damages it could do.

"haven't you ever wanted to love someone and not feel some type of pain?" he asked.

"not really," she responded, "i've always found that the pain is apart of love, and the more you try and avoid it, the more it increases."

love without some type of struggle is like the night sky without the stars and moon: plain, boring, and dark, oh so dark.

a life without pain & discomfort is a life without
knowledge.
a life without growth.

i've saved you an apartment in my heart that is marked with your handprints, which you may always come back to whenever you have nowhere else to go or if you just want to say hi.

-you will always be welcome in my heart

perhaps she was too strong to not be broken.

when i was young everyone looked down on me like i
was a clown house in a neighborhood of castles,
but now that i am grown,
everyone cranes their necks looking up at my skyscraper
surrounded by their sheds.

mosaics, i have come to find, are a lot like people. from afar, it looks like a regular picture, a splendid piece of lavishing art. but, when looking closer, the mosaic is made up of millions of small, broken pieces. despite its un-completeness, it is still beautiful.

despite your mending and broken pieces,
you are still just as beautiful.

everything worthy of beauty is compiled of broken art.

no matter how much i succeed and fly,
no matter how high i get,
i hope i will always stay grounded.
i hope the areoplane's height will not
heighten my ego.

love someone = love the universe.
A whole galaxy of endless stars in their eyes that the
world has sculpted:
looking up at the galaxy of a milky way of asteroids in
the sky the world has painted.
If the world created me, then am I apart of the world's
beauty or am I the beauty of the world?

know someone = know the world.
To see both hurricanes and rainbows and understand that
each must occur,
like the way someone fights and cries but must also
bloom and shine,
out-bursting a million beautiful colors from their
waterfall of tears.
If the world created me, then are the lines on my palms a
map of the world's brokenness
or are they the lines of my own cracks the world has
instilled in me to put back together?

hurt someone = hurt the universe,
saying as if the world did not know what it was doing by
putting "your ugly self on it."
If the world created me, then when they hurt me with
their cracked hands and suffocating words, are they
hurting the world or are they hurting themselves?

I love myself by loving the world.
It's a full circle of endless love and growth, if you ponder
on it for too long you'll understand it.
We walk around wearing an emotional disguise

- a barrier between the people around us and who we
really are-
because of the fear of others, fear of what people might
do if they were to truly see us.
Afraid of what they might think of our loving hearts the
world has so carefully given,
we hide away in the dark, wishing for their words and
hits to end.

Take off your mask and the world shall do the same
Shine your heart for the world to see and the world shall
shine its' sun and moon for you to see, just as beautiful.
Love yourself and the world shall do the same.
If the world created me, and if I love myself, then do I
thank the world for what it has done for me or does the
world silently thank me?

The universe has taught me that the true love is in the
bravery to become my real self,
the self I have been hiding for so long,
the self the world made me to be.

love someone = love this planet and everything it offers.
love the world = love myself and everything I am.

love someone = love yourself.

if something is lost it can always be found.
but sometimes it is not meant to be found.
sometimes the greatest gift you can ever receive
is losing and not finding.

in chess, the Pawn may become the Queen.
first, the piece must get to the other side and fight its way
through,
but the little one can become the big one.

"you are to die for," he said.
"no," she responded.

"i am the reason to live for."

not everyone can love the sunshine,
even if it is essential to life

but, my darling, the stars do not shine for you,
or me, or anyone.
the stars shine for themselves.
they aren't afraid to show the world who they really are
and neither should you.

shine for yourself, because you can.

All day long, I walked alone. Somehow, I ended up at the sea. I wonder if anyone has felt this before.
The weight on my eyes from this entire world captures my attention.
I see the horizon; it's calling my name.

Why isn't life one straight line like the horizon?
Can anyone hear me?

The sea is so much bigger than me, but my dreams are bigger. I don't know how to swim, but I know how to walk. So, if I can't reach you soon, I'll eventually get there.
The world is quiet. The world is my home. I am floating in the sea. I don't know how to swim, but I know how to fly; if I could only reach the sky.
The horizon - the line where blue meets blue - is now staring at me. It wonders how I have managed to get myself here. It wonders how I have strayed off path so far. It laughs at me for not being like it: so smooth and consistent, so predictable with its straight line of blue.
My site has gone hazy, but I can make out my dreams in the distance. Even if I stray off this path more, I know I'll end up where I should be. I don't know how to swim, but I know how to believe.

I'm standing on the intertidal zone - the line where ocean meets land - I see the world. I see myself. I believe in myself.

I am now leaning over the water. Seeing my reflection in

the wide sea, I face my wavering self.

The self I have always wanted to meet; the self the world sees me as.

The self that is winding levels and twisting journeys.

they say if you love something,
you should set it free.

so i let myself go.

Ella Shutze

i'm scared for you,
because you're scared
of being scared.

when the pain is stronger than the love,
let your pain become your savior.

And in that moment of final defeat and struggle, she found herself. She found her strength again, and she rose stronger, more powerful than before. For she knew who she was now, and she would never go back. The devil was still apart of her, and maybe it will always be. But she was stronger than the Narcissism; she was stronger than those who disliked her. For she knew who she was, and she knew that if she were to ever lose herself and this world again that it would be okay, because being lost is not bad. Being lost could be the greatest gift you ever received.

She knew that if you wanted to truly create yourself, you had to first lose yourself,

over and over again.

With a final look in the cracked mirror, I hold my breath.
My mask in my hand, I raise my eyes to the sky. The
stars shine on my scars, and the moon smiles at my
vulnerable soul.
The wind kisses my check and whispers in my ear how
proud she is of my disheveled hair.

The Devil and Angel were now a mere, faint memory,
neither one of them more important than the other.

Even though the Devil can be ruinous, he can also be
beautiful.

don't push the pain away;
feel everything,
and
carry on.

all of this hurting won't be for nothing.

38565700R00100

Made in the USA
Columbia, SC
05 December 2018